FARMS

# Chicken Farms

Ann Thomas

MACMILLAN

Acknowledgements

With special thanks to T.L.B. for all the time and effort.

Thanks to the Victorian Egg Producers Co-operative.

The author and publishers are grateful to the following for permission to reproduce copyright material.

Cover: Australian Picture Library

Kathie Atkinson, p. 14; Australian Picture Library, pp. 6, 29 © Nick Rains; G. I. Bernard/OSF, pp. 15, 26; Coo-ee Picture Library, pp. 12, 13, 20, 24, 25, 27; Robert Dowling/OSF, p. 30; Great Southern Stock, pp. 5, 11, 28; Graham Meadows Photography, pp. 8, 10, 16, 17, 19, 21, 22; Stock Photos/Owen Hughes, p. 4. .

While every care has been taken to trace and acknowledge copyright, the publishers tender their apologies for any accidental infringement where copyright has proved untraceable.



First published 1998 by
MACMILLAN EDUCATION AUSTRALIA PTY LTD
627 Chapel Street, South Yarra 3141
Reprinted 1999

Associated companies and representatives throughout the world

National Library of Australia cataloguing in publication data

Thomas, Ann
Chicken farms.

Includes index.
ISBN 0 7329 4374 4.

1. Chickens – Juvenile literature. 2. Farms – Juvenile literature. I. Title. (Series : Farms).

636.5

Text design by Polar Design
Cover design by Linda Forss
Typeset in Officinaprim by Alena Jencik of Grand Graphix Pty Ltd
Printed in Hong Kong

# Contents

# What is a farm?

Land can be used to grow crops or raise animals. This land is called a farm.

People who work on farms are called farmers.
There are many different types of farm.

# Chicken farms

Farms where chickens are raised are called chicken farms. Chicken farms produce eggs and chickens.

The eggs are used for eating or for **hatching** more chickens. The chickens are used as meat for people and animals to eat.

## Different ways to farm chickens

There are four types of chicken farm. Each type of farm raises chickens in different ways but for the same purposes.

Chicken farms raise chickens for eggs and for meat.

*Battery farming*

Battery chicken farms keep chickens in small cages. It is easy to collect eggs, keep them clean and to feed and inspect the hens.

## *Controlled environment farming*

Some chickens are farmed in large sheds, in a controlled environment. These sheds have no windows. The sheds have lights. Air is pumped into the sheds.

The chickens can walk around in the shed. The floor is covered with a deep layer of wood shavings or straw or rice **hulls**. The hens lay their eggs in nesting boxes in the shed.

### *Open shed farming*

Some chickens are farmed in open-sided sheds. These sheds have large windows or shutters to let in light and air.

The chickens live in cages or in deep litter.

## *Free-range farming*

During the day, free-range chickens wander and scratch in large pens or paddocks. Chickens are locked in sheds at night to keep them safe from **predators** and the weather.

The hens lay their eggs in nesting boxes in the shed.

# Which chickens?

Chickens are used for different purposes. Some chickens are raised as **meat birds**. Meat birds are often called broilers.

These birds have more **flesh**, are usually heavier, have good straight legs and an even breast bone.

Some chickens are raised for egg laying. These hens lay about five eggs each week.

That means a chicken can lay 260 eggs in a year. These birds are not so meaty and people do not eat them. They are usually used for pet food when they are no longer used for laying eggs.

# Feeding

Chickens eat different foods at different times in their lives. Young chicks eat starter crumble, full of vitamins and minerals.

Older chickens eat special pellets of wheat, grains, vitamins and minerals. Egg-laying chickens eat production pellets to help them lay larger, healthier eggs. Free-range chickens have pellets as well as wheat, food scraps, insects and greens from scratching outdoors.

Chickens have no teeth. They have a special area called a crop where they grind their food.

They swallow tiny stones or shell grit with their food. These stones and grit rub against the food, breaking it into smaller pieces. The chicken can then **digest** the food properly.

# Diseases

Farmers work hard to keep their chickens free from disease. Farmers put medicine into their chickens' food and water to stop them from getting fowl pox, viral infections and other diseases.

Medicine is put into tanks which hold drinking water for chickens.

Chicken sheds are cleaned often to keep out insects, mice and rats and to cut down on disease.

# Eggs

Pullets are young chickens which have not laid an egg yet. When pullets are ready to lay eggs, they are trained to use nesting boxes. Most birds have a favourite nest they like to lay their eggs in.

Eggs are collected daily. They are inspected, sorted by weight and size and put into boxes. These are the eggs we buy at the shops.

# Meat

When a chicken can no longer lay eggs or when it is just over one year old, it is killed. Some farmers kill, clean and process their own chickens.

Other farmers send their live chickens to processing plants. Here, meat workers kill the chickens and prepare them for sale in the shops.

# Special chickens

Some farmers breed chickens for their looks. These birds take part in competitions. They may be extra big, extra small, have brightly coloured feathers or have other special features.

Bantam hen (above)

Gold silkies (below)

# Glossary

**digest** to soften and change food in the stomach so the body can use the vitamins and minerals

**flesh** body meat

**hatching** young chickens coming out of eggs

**hulls** husks or outside covering of seeds and grains

**meat birds** chickens bred to have more meat on their bodies; chickens for eating

**predators** animals that hunt or kill other animals for food

# Index